1

T5-AQT-436

POWER

"I can do all things through Christ which strengtheneth me."

–Philippians 4:13
The Holy Bible

Power Is The Ability To Walk Away
From Something You Desire
To Protect Something Else You Love.

-MIKE MURDOCK

2

ABUSE

"So that we may boldly say, The Lord is my helper, and I will not fear what man shall do unto me."

–Hebrews 13:6
The Holy Bible

Never Complain About What You Permit.

-MIKE MURDOCK

3

ANGER

"Wherefore, my beloved brethren, let every man be swift to hear, slow to speak, slow to wrath: For the wrath of man worketh not the righteousness of God."

–James 1:19,20
The Holy Bible

Anger Is Simply Passion Requiring An Appropriate Focus.

-MIKE MURDOCK

4

DATING

"Be ye not unequally yoked together with unbelievers: for what fellowship hath righteousness with unrighteousness? and what communion hath light with darkness?"

–2 Corinthians 6:14
The Holy Bible

Nobody Is Ever As They First Appear.

-MIKE MURDOCK

5

CHANGE

"Therefore if any man be in Christ, he is a new creature: old things are passed away; behold, all things are become new."

-2 Corinthians 5:17
The Holy Bible

Men Do Not Drown By Falling In Water But By Staying There.

-MIKE MURDOCK

CHOICES

"I call heaven and earth to record this day against you, that I have set before you life and death, blessing and cursing: therefore choose life, that both thou and thy seed may live:"

–Deuteronomy 30:19
The Holy Bible

Your Decisions Decide Your Joy.
-MIKE MURDOCK

7

CHURCH

"Not forsaking the assembling of ourselves together, as the manner of some is; but exhorting one another: and so much the more, as ye see the day approaching."

–Hebrews 10:25
The Holy Bible

The Climate Around You Determines The Power That Grows Within You.

-MIKE MURDOCK

8

WISDOM

"Wisdom is the principal thing; therefore get wisdom: and with all thy getting get understanding."

–Proverbs 4:7
The Holy Bible

Every Problem In Your Life Is Simply A Wisdom Problem.

-MIKE MURDOCK

CRISIS

"And we know that all things work together for good to them that love God, to them who are the called according to His purpose."

–Romans 8:28
The Holy Bible

Crisis Is The School Where Your Greatness Is Born.

-MIKE MURDOCK

10

DEPRESSION

"...weeping may endure for a night, but joy cometh in the morning."

–Psalm 30:5
The Holy Bible

Your Focus Decides Your Feelings.

-MIKE MURDOCK

FAITH

"For verily I say unto you, That whosoever shall say unto this mountain, Be thou removed, and be thou cast into the sea; and shall not doubt in his heart, but shall believe that those things which he saith shall come to pass; he shall have whatsoever he saith."

–Mark 11:23
The Holy Bible

What You Say Reveals What You Believe.

-MIKE MURDOCK

12

FEAR

"For God hath not given us the spirit of fear; but of power, and of love, and of a sound mind."

–2 Timothy 1:7
The Holy Bible

You Can Only Conquer What You Are Willing To Confront.

-MIKE MURDOCK

13

FORGETTING THE PAST

"Remember ye not the former things, neither consider the things of old."

-Isaiah 43:18
The Holy Bible

Stop Discussing What You Want Others To Forget.

-MIKE MURDOCK

14

FORGIVENESS

"But if ye do not forgive, neither will your Father which is in heaven forgive your trespasses."

–Mark 11:26
The Holy Bible

Your Forgiveness Of Others Determines God's Forgiveness Of You. -MIKE MURDOCK

15

STUDYING YOUR BIBLE

"Study to shew thyself approved unto God, a workman that needeth not to be ashamed, rightly dividing the word of truth."

–2 Timothy 2:15
The Holy Bible

The Word Of God Is The Wisdom Of God.

-MIKE MURDOCK

16

HONORING YOUR PARENTS

"Honour thy father and mother; That it may be well with thee, and thou mayest live long on the earth."

–Ephesians 6:2,3
The Holy Bible

Your Reaction To Your Parents Determines God's Reaction To You. *-MIKE MURDOCK*

17

JEALOUSY

"Let us not be desirous of vain glory, provoking one another, envying one another."

–Galatians 5:26
The Holy Bible

Jealousy Occurs When You Believe Someone Else Received What You Earned.   *-MIKE MURDOCK*

18

LAZINESS

"...if any would not work, neither should he eat."

–2 Thessalonians 3:10

The Holy Bible

The Problems You Solve Determine The Rewards You Receive. *-MIKE MURDOCK*

19

LONELINESS

"...for He hath said, I will never leave thee, nor forsake thee."

–Hebrews 13:5
The Holy Bible

Loneliness Is Not The Absence Of Affection But The Absence Of Direction. *-MIKE MURDOCK*

20

LOVE OF GOD

"For I am persuaded, that
neither death, nor life, nor
angels, nor principalities, nor
powers, nor things present, nor
things to come, Nor height, nor
depth, nor any other creature,
shall be able to separate us
from the love of God, which is
in Christ Jesus our Lord."

–Romans 8:38,39
The Holy Bible

The Hatred Of Satan Toward You
Can Not Compare With The Love
Of God Toward You. *-MIKE MURDOCK*

21

SUCCESS

"But seek ye first the kingdom of God, and His right-eousness; and all these things shall be added unto you."

-Matthew 6:33
The Holy Bible

Your Success Is Determined By What You Are Willing To Ignore. -MIKE MURDOCK

22

LYING

"These six things doth the Lord hate: yea, seven are an abomination unto Him: A proud look, a lying tongue, and hands that shed innocent blood, An heart that deviseth wicked imaginations, feet that be swift in running to mischief,"

–Proverbs 6:16-18
The Holy Bible

Those Who Will Lie For You Will Eventually Lie About You.
-MIKE MURDOCK

23

MISTAKES

"For a just man falleth seven times, and riseth up again: but the wicked shall fall into mischief."

–Proverbs 24:16
The Holy Bible

All Men Fall, The Great Ones Get Back Up.

-MIKE MURDOCK

24

PATIENCE

"And let us not be weary in well doing: for in due season we shall reap, if we faint not."

–Galatians 6:9
The Holy Bible

Waiting Is The Proof Of Trust.

-MIKE MURDOCK

25

PEOPLE PRESSURE

"My son, if sinners entice thee, consent thou not. My son, walk not thou in the way with them; refrain thy foot from their path:"

–Proverbs 1:10,15
The Holy Bible

Those Who Sin With You Eventually Sin Against You.

-MIKE MURDOCK

26

PRAYER

"Confess your faults
one to another, and
pray one for another,
that ye may be healed.
The effectual fervent
prayer of a righteous
man availeth much."

–James 5:16
The Holy Bible

One Hour In The Presence Of
God Will Reveal Any Flaw In Your
Most Carefully Laid Plans.

-MIKE MURDOCK

27

REJECTION

"When my father and my mother forsake me, then the Lord will take me up."

–Psalm 27:10
The Holy Bible

Those Who Create Your Pain Today Do Not Control The Successes Of Your Future.

-MIKE MURDOCK

28

RENEWING YOUR MIND

"And be not conformed to this world: but be ye transformed by the renewing of your mind, that ye may prove what is that good, and acceptable, and perfect, will of God."

–Romans 12:2
The Holy Bible

The Battle Of Life Is In Your Mind; The Battle Of The Mind Is For Your Focus. -MIKE MURDOCK

29

TITHING

"Give, and it shall be given unto you; good measure, pressed down, and shaken together, and running over, shall men give into your bosom. For with the same measure that ye mete withal it shall be measured to you again."

–Luke 6:38
The Holy Bible

Seed-Faith Is Sowing What You Have Been Given To Create What You Have Been Promised.

-MIKE MURDOCK

- 29 -

SELF-CONFIDENCE

"I will praise Thee; for I am fearfully and wonderfully made: marvellous are Thy works; and that my soul knoweth right well."

–Psalm 139:14
The Holy Bible

Your Significance Is Not In Your Similarity To Another But In Your Point Of Difference From Another.

-MIKE MURDOCK

31

SEXUAL TEMPTATION

"Blessed is the man that endureth temptation: for when he is tried, he shall receive the crown of life, which the Lord hath promised to them that love Him."

–James 1:12
The Holy Bible

Those Who Create Your Guilt Have Sabotaged Your Trust.
-MIKE MURDOCK

DECISION

Will You Accept Jesus As Your Personal Savior Today?

The Bible says, "That if thou shalt confess with thy mouth the Lord Jesus, and shalt believe in thine heart that God hath raised Him from the dead, thou shalt be saved" (Romans 10:9).

Pray this prayer from your heart today! *"Dear Jesus, I believe that You died for me and rose again on the third day. I confess I am a sinner...I need Your love and forgiveness...Come into my heart. Forgive my sins. I receive Your eternal life. Confirm Your love by giving me peace, joy and supernatural love for others. Amen."*

☐ Yes, Mike! I made a decision to accept Christ as my personal Savior today. Please send me my free gift of your book *"31 Keys To A New Beginning"* to help me with my new life in Christ. *(B-48)*

NAME _____

ADDRESS _____

CITY _____ STATE _____ ZIP _____

PHONE ( ) _____ E-MAIL _____

Mail To: **The Wisdom Center**
P.O. Box 99 · Denton, TX 76202
1-888-WISDOM-1 (1-888-947-3661)
Website: thewisdomcenter.tv

Clip and Mail

Unless otherwise indicated, all Scripture quotations are taken from the King James Version of the Bible.
31 Scriptures Every Teen Should Memorize · ISBN 1-56394-229-1/B-185
Copyright © 1994 by **MIKE MURDOCK**
All publishing rights belong exclusively to Wisdom International
Publisher/Editor: Deborah Murdock Johnson
Published by The Wisdom Center · P.O. Box 99 · Denton, Texas 76202
1-888-WISDOM-1 (1-888-947-3661) · **Website: thewisdomcenter.tv**
Printed in the United States of America. All rights reserved under International Copyright Law. Contents and/or cover may not be reproduced in whole or in part in any form without the expressed written consent of the publisher.   030405K